Downton Abbey

Your Backstage Pass to the Era and
Making of the TV Series

Jessica Long

As a "thank you" for purchasing this book I want to give you a gift. It is 100% absolutely free.

Please go to http://fandomkindlebooks.com/downton-abbey-bonus/ to discover more fascinating facts about Downton Abbey and the smash hit BBC TV series.

Disclaimer

Other Books in the British TV Drama & Movie Series

Available on Kindle and in paperback on Amazon

Call The Midwife!: Your Backstage Pass to the Era and the Making of the PBS TV Series

Doctor Who: 200 Facts on the Characters and Making of the BBC TV Series

Mr Selfridge: Your Backstage Pass to the True Harry Selfridge Story and Making of the PBS TV Series

Pride & Prejudice: Your Backstage Pass to Jane Austen's Novel and The Making of the BBC TV Series, Starring Colin Firth

Sherlock Lives! 100+ Facts on Sherlock and the Smash Hit BBC TV Series

The Bletchley Park Enigma: 200+ Facts on the Story of Alan Turing That Inspired The Smash Hit Movie "The Imitation Game" Starring Benedict Cumberbatch

<u>Books in the Royals and Celebrities series</u>

KATE: Loyal Wife, Royal Mother, Queen-In-Waiting

HARRY: Popstar Prince

One Direction: Your Backstage Pass To The Boys, The Band, And The 1D Phenomenon

Spoiler Alert

Every effort has been made to avoid spoilers for the latest season, Season 4. If you have watched to the end of Season 3, you can read this without encountering Season 4 plotlines.

However, if you are not current with your viewing of Downton Abbey, I suggest you wait on reading this book until you have reached the end of Season 3.

Table of Contents

Introduction

Downton Abbey first appeared on TV screens in the UK in September 2010 and the US in January 2011.

It quickly became a firm favorite with its fans with its depiction of life in a stately home in the early 1900's, both above and below stairs.

Its success is almost definitely down to the intrigue the two very different lifestyles create. Upstairs, it is a life of luxury, of opulence, of social class and reputation.

Below stairs there is also a hierarchy, but life is tough and rewards very few. If you were lucky, you could work your way up the ranks of domestic service and stay with one family throughout your career, maybe even earning a retirement at the end of it.

If you were unlucky you stayed at the bottom of the ladder, destined to scrub floors and work long hours every day, with little time off and even less chance of security at the end of it.

Simply put, Downton Abbey is about people whose lives, their opportunities, or lack of them, are determined by the position they were born into.

Downton Abbey succeeds in bringing the drama of a large Edwardian house to life. As viewers, we are as hooked on the stories of the servants below stairs as we are on the dramas playing out above them.

Writer and creator, Julian Fellowes, draws us into a world gone by. A time of extreme contrast between the haves and the have-nots.

Come with me as I take you on a journey to Downton Abbey. Let's weave our way through the great halls and majestic grandeur that is home to the Crawley family and their servants.

Background

Writer

Writer and creator, Julian Fellowes, is also responsible for the 2001 film 'Gosford Park'. Fellowes won an Oscar for 'Best Screenplay Written Directly for the Screen' for 'Gosford Park'.

As well as being a screenwriter, Fellowes is also an actor, director and novelist.

His wife, Emma Joy Kitchener Fellowes, has been chief lady-in-waiting* to HRH Princess Michael of Kent for 25 years.

*Fellowes, a Conservative party member of parliament, is also a member of the House of Lords.***

The first series of Downton Abbey opens with the death of the heir of the Crawley family, aboard the Titanic. Fellowes wrote a mini-series on the disaster, that was shown on British TV in the Spring of 2012.

Notes:

*Lady-in-waiting – a female assistant in a royal court. She would attend a queen, princess or noblewomen of high standing. Typically, she would be of a high ranking family herself, although not as high as the woman she tended to.

**House of Lords – is the upper house of the parliamentary system of the United Kingdom. Unlike the House of Commons, where members are elected, most new members are 'life peers' appointed by the Monarch on the advice of the Prime Minister.

Locations

Filming for Downton Abbey takes place in several locations around the UK.

The exterior shots of Downton Abbey come from Highclere Castle in Hampshire.

Much of the interior is also shot in Highclere Castle, although the servant's quarters, kitchens and several of the upstairs bedrooms, are filmed on set at Ealing Studios, London.

Outdoor scenes are filmed in the Oxfordshire village of Bampton.

The exterior of Isobel Crawley's house is filmed at the old rectory in Bampton, whilst the interior scenes were shot at Hall Place, near Beaconsfield in Buckinghamshire.

The second series takes us through the First World War. The trench scenes were filmed in specially constructed trenches in a field outside the village of Akenham in Suffolk.

Life Above Stairs

Class system was everything back in the early 1900's. There were three very distinct classes; Upper, Middle and Lower class. You did not tend to mix outside your class.

The Upper Class tended to be 'inherited wealth' and would certainly have included some of the oldest families in the country. Many of them would have been titled.

Pastimes for men would have included the traditions of hunting, shooting and fishing. Horse riding would also have been a favorite pursuit for leisure and in competition.

Women were expected to make good marriages, which were often arranged. Most young girls would dream of nothing else but meeting their beau and living in wedded bliss.

If a woman wanted to pursue a career, it is likely that she would have remained single. Married women did not work, unless they were very poor.

Once married, a young woman would have staff to look after her house, nannies for her babies and young children. Her time would have been pretty much her own.

The women would spend their days visiting each other or indulging in needlework, crafts and music. These were activities that were considered 'womanly and gentle'.

Life Below Stairs

The largest form of employment for working class women in the early 1900's would have been as a domestic servant.

Being a servant meant that there were plenty of rules to be obeyed. You NEVER spoke to a member of the house unless there was a specific reason to, and you kept it as brief as possible.

If you passed one of the members of the house in a corridor, you would turn to the wall, attempting to make yourself as invisible as you could.

When walking with a member of the house, a servant was always expected to walk several paces behind.

Senior servants had more power and wielded this over the staff below them. For instance, if the butler finished his meal and put down his cutlery, everyone else would be expected to follow suit. You learned to become a fast eater!

Working hours were long, anything up to 17 hours. Time off was scarce, usually one evening a week and every other Sunday.

Characters and Actors

Above Stairs

Robert Crawley, Earl of Grantham

Born in Downton Abbey, Robert is the son of the previous Earl of Grantham* and his wife Violet the present Dowager Countess.

As was normal for this period, he was brought up by his nanny, spending just an hour a day with his mother.

Robert also has a sister, Rosamund, and at least two aunts and a cousin.

His father had little money for an aristocrat with property the size of Downton Abbey, and so Robert knew from a young age that he would be expected to marry a wealthy heiress.

Writer Julian Fellowes has stated that the character of Robert Crawley is based on his own father, 'a deeply moral man'.

Despite the fact that Robert does make bad investments, which put Downton Abbey in jeopardy, his loyalty to his family never falters.

Notes:

*Earl – an Earl is in theory the ruler of the county. The old name for an Earl used to be a Count. Nowadays, the title is simply that, a title.

Hugh Bonneville (Earl of Grantham)

Hugh began his acting career in 1986, having a successful stage

career for some 10 years before transitioning to TV and film.

He had roles in the big screen films, 'Notting Hill' and 'Tomorrow Never Dies'

He has received both Emmy and Golden Globe nominations for his portrayal of Robert Crawley.

'The most humane of writers' is how Bonneville describes director and writer Julian Fellowes.

He says this of fellow actor Maggie Smith; 'Once off camera, she's naughty, funny, and is the mistress of the flinty stare delicately edged with a twinkle'.

His favorite room in Highclere Castle is the library. His least favorite is the dining room, as meals always take so long to shoot.

He admits to there being an element of 'fantasy' about playing the Lord of Downton Abbey. Driving up to Highclere Castle, whenever he filmed there, would make his heart flutter!

Cora Crawley, Countess of Grantham

Lord Grantham initially marries Cora in order to secure the future of Downton Abbey. As part of the marriage, Cora has to sign over her fortune to the family. How much she is worth is never established.

Because daughters could inherit neither titles nor wealth, the only way to ensure Cora's title is passed down to her eldest daughter is to have her marry the heir to the Grantham fortune, Patrick Crawley.

Cora was from Cincinnati and was the only daughter and child of the dry goods multi-millionaire Isidore Levinson.

She was part of a wave of wealthy young women known as the "Buccaneers" who came over to marry British aristocrats. In so doing, they purchased respect-ability while their new husbands gained access to the cash necessary to support their crumbling estates.

Probably the most famous "Buccaneer" was Lady Randolph Churchill, born Jeanette Jerome, who became the mother of British Prime Minister, Winston Churchill.

Cora's mother brings her to London in 1888 for her first season** and it is here that she meets Robert Crawley.

Cora is a sweet and gentle-natured woman, choosing to see the good in the people around her. She can be gullible, however, and her tendency to see the good in others can cause her to be blind to the bad.

Fellowes found the inspiration for Cora partly in the American Mary Leiter. Through her marriage to George Curzon, Mary became Baroness*** Curzon of Kedleston and Vicereine**** of India.

Notes:

*Countess – the wife of the Earl.

**Season – the social season was an annual event, whereby, all the elite from society would gather in London for parties, dinners and charitable events. It was deemed a good opportunity for 'young la-dies' to meet their future spouses.

***Baroness – the wife of a Baron. A Baron was one of the lower ranks of nobility.

****Vicereine – the wife of a Viceroy. A Viceroy is an official who runs a country, colony or city province on behalf of his Monarch.

Elizabeth McGovern (Cora, Countess of Grantham)

Elizabeth has received critical acclaim for her role as Cora, many believing that she is the biggest stand-out from the show.

She has been nominated for both an Emmy and a Golden Globe for her role in the show.

Elizabeth sings lead vocals in a folk group called 'Sadie and the Hotheads'.

Michelle Dockery, who plays Cora's daughter Mary in the show, also sometimes sings with the group.

Gillian Anderson (X Files) was reportedly offered the part of Cora and turned it down before it went to Elizabeth.

Elizabeth has lived in London, UK, since 1982.

Violet Crawley, Dowager Countess* of Grantham

Violet was born the daughter of a Baronet**. Although her family were titled, they were not of money and she brought only a title with her to the marriage with the 4ᵗʰ Earl of Grantham.

As a young girl in the 1850's and 60's, Violet would have worn the 'bustle*** and crinoline.'****

Violet was against Robert's marriage to Cora, however, she did reap the financial benefits that Cora's fortune brought to the Crawley family.

Violet uses her cunning to manipulate people to her way of thinking. She likes to keep a firm control on all situations.

She will go to lengths to protect the honor of her family and stop them becoming the topic of idle gossip.

Julian Fellowes has twice used his great-aunt Isie as the basis of his characters. Firstly as Lady Trentham in 'Gosford Park', and secondly as Violet Crawley. The actress Maggie Smith plays both roles.

Notes:

*Dowager Countess – is a widow who holds title or property left by her husband.

**Baronet – the rank below Baron, but one above a Knight.

***Bustle – a bustle was a framework worn at the back of a woman's dress at the waist. It helped support the weight of the fabric which otherwise would have dragged and fallen flat.

****Crinoline – was a stiff structure worn as an undergarment, to support the weight of the skirts that were the fashion at the time.

Maggie Smith (Dowager Countess)

Maggie Smith's career has spanned over 60 years and she has won numerous awards for her role as Violet Crawley. Over her career, she's won two Oscars, three Emmys and a Tony, plus many other awards.

She is well known for her role as Professor Minerva McGonagal in the Harry Potter films.

In 1990 she was given the title 'Dame'*.

She won her two Oscars for her roles in 'The Prime of Miss Jean Brodie' and 'Californian Suite'.

Her personal life hasn't always been straightforward. While waiting for her fiancé's divorce to come through, she met and married Robert Stevens. Nine years later, two years after her own divorce from Stevens, she married her original fiancé, Bev-

erley Cross, to whom she was married until his death twenty-three years later. She had first met him when she was 18.

She has two sons, both of whom are actors. One of them, Toby Stevens, has admitted that he doesn't like to watch Downton Abbey.

It would seem to run in the family, as Maggie herself also admits to not watching the show. Her reasons are that 'she always sees something that she thinks she should have done differently'. She performs for 'the delight of acting' and not to see the finished product.

The cast of Downton Abbey like to play Bananagrams in between takes. According to Allen Leech who plays estate manager Tom Branson, Dame Maggie is "the champion". He says, "She's one of the wittiest and most intelligent women I've ever met. You can't beat her. Her vocabulary would knock you for six. She does The Times crossword."

Dame Maggie was told by her grandmother that she wasn't pretty enough to be an actress and should learn to type.

Dame Maggie is a breast cancer survivor. She has spoken of how it shocked her and caused a loss of confidence, although she also had a sense of humor about it. She continued to shoot a Harry Potter film during treatment. "I was hairless. I had no problem getting the wig on. I was like a boiled egg."

She's known for her colourful language.

She has renounced retirement saying, "I'll keep going with Violet and whatever other old biddy comes along.'

Notes:

*The title "Dame" is the female equivalent of the rank of Knighthood in the British honors system.

Isobel Crawley

Isobel is the widowed mother of Matthew Crawley who will later learn that by some fluke, he is to inherit Downton Abbey.

Isobel husband and father were both doctors and she, herself, is a trained nurse. This makes her a member of the professional middle class.

She holds a very different set of values from the family at Downton Abbey. It is important to her that she helps those less fortunate than herself and her character is imbued with the need to take on responsibilities, at times irritating those around her with her zealousness.

It is this need that sees her persuading the Countess to allow the Abbey to be converted to a hospital during the war and performing a multitude of "good deeds" throughout the show.

Underneath this caring, "do-gooding" exterior she is essentially a lonely woman whose practical nature makes it difficult to form relationships. She adores her only child, Matthew, and therefore is devastated when he dies.

She has an ongoing rivalry with the Dowager Countess which plays out as a "war of words" and there is plenty of witty repartee between these two characters that render many of the best one-liners in the show.

Penelope Wilton (Isobel Crawley)

Penelope Wilton is a highly acclaimed British actress of TV, stage and film. Her career has spanned forty years.

She is perhaps best known to US audiences as activist Wendy Woods in the movie Cry Freedom.

She appeared in *Doctor Who* as Harriet, a Member of Parliament, a part especially written for her, and the comedy *Ever Decreasing Circles* with Richard Briers.

She is very friendly with Dame Maggie Smith and they appeared in a film together, The Best Exotic Marigold Hotel.

While filming *The Best Exotic Marigold Hotel*, Penelope, Dame Maggie and Judi Dench would play Bananagrams and she too espouses Dame Maggie's skill at the game.

She has said that she would like her character if she met her in real-life, "Julian Fellowes has written a very interesting woman, who is probably led by her heart quite a lot of the time but who nowadays would probably be doing something a bit more fulfilling because women didn't have jobs like they do now. She would be a career woman and would probably be editing The Guardian women's page. She would be doing something forward-thinking... she's a bit of a lefty. I like her very much."

Lady Mary Crawley (Michelle Dockery)

Because she is a woman, Mary cannot inherit the title of Countess of Grantham on her father's death. However, as the eldest of three girls and with no male siblings, she should have been able to inherit Downton Abbey and any monies. Her grandfather stopped this from being a possibility when he linked the property to the title. This meant that only a male heir could inherit. This is why Mary has to marry the next male heir to Downton, in order to become the next Countess.

When her husband, her fourth cousin Matthew Crawley, dies in a road accident, Mary misses out on becoming Countess. Instead, the title now moves to her son George.

Michelle Dockery who is cast as Lady Mary comes from humble beginnings. She had to scrimp and save to attend London's renowned Guildhall School of Music and Drama working as a waitress and in offices.

Michelle is from Dagenham, London and sometimes surprises fans in real-life when her accent isn't as cut-glass as her on-screen character, Lady Mary. She says, "I'm an actress. That's my job yet people are surprised when I don't sound like Lady Mary."

Her big film breakout is *Non-Stop* with Liam Neeson and Julianne Moore released February 2014.

Michelle is a jazz singer and sang at Ronnie Scott's Jazz Club in London, 2009. As mentioned above she has performed with Elizabeth McGovern's band, Sadie and the Hotheads.

Matthew Crawley (Dan Stevens)

Upon the death of Patrick Crawley, Robert writes a letter to Matthew informing him that he is now the heir to Downton Abbey and will be the 6th Earl of Grantham. Initially he tries to refuse, worried that he will be made to marry one of Roberts's three daughters.

After much trauma between them, Mary and Matthew eventually marry and have a son. Their happiness is short lived, as on his return to Downton Abbey from visiting Mary and their newborn son in hospital, he is killed in a road accident.

Dan Stevens, the actor who played Matthew Crawley, recently admitted that he spent 2013 apologizing to people for ruining their Christmas Day. (The episode which ended with Matthew's death aired at the end of the Christmas TV special in the UK.)

Dan and Michelle Dockery (Lady Mary) first appeared together in the television movie, "The Turn of the Screw". Set in London in 1921, she plays a young governess and he her psychiatrist.

He is married with two children and currently based in New York. He says he's always wanted to live in New York but misses his friends and a good curry.

Lady Edith Crawley (Laura Carmichael)

As the middle daughter, Edith feels she is lost between her pretty, smooth-talking elder sister Mary and her passionate and daring younger sister Sybil.

Edith has a difficult time with suitors. She truly loves the heir to Downton Abbey, Patrick Crawley, but her elder sister has first claim. Patrick is then killed aboard the Titanic leaving Edith desolate. She is then jilted at the altar and her luck doesn't change when she falls in love with newspaper editor Michael Gregson. Gregson truly loves her but has a difficult background, being married to a woman who is now in a lunatic asylum.

Like her character, Laura Carmichael is the middle of three sisters. She has said they don't have nearly the nasty relationship as the one she has with her on-screen sisters.

Before appearing in Downton Abbey, Laura was a jobbing actor and was waiting to hear if she would be offered a part in Twelfth Night in Dubai. She turned the Shakespearean role down to hang on to hear about Downton, working as a receptionist while doing so.

She says of working on Downton Abbey, "Downton has been such a big break for me. I'm completely spoiled. My first scene was with Hugh Bonneville, my second was with Jim Carter, my third was with Maggie Smith. What can I say?"

Laura loves the quintessential British snack, Twiglets.

Lady Sybil Benson (Jessica Brown-Findlay)

The youngest of the Crawley sisters and something of a family rebel, Sybil seems to get away with more than her two siblings. Politically conscious, her standing within the aristocracy means less to her than marrying for true love.

Sybil falls in love with the family's chauffeur and runs away to marry him. They return to gain approval of the family and then leave to live in Ireland. However, they move back to Downton when Cora learns she is to be a grandmother. She tells Robert that she cannot bear to be parted from her daughter and grandchild and so he allows them back.

However, Sybil dies from complications following childbirth amid much wailing from die-hard fans. Her plight caused the profile of the condition pre-eclampsia to be raised – even the **Washington Post** ran an article on it.

The part of Lady Sybil was written out of the series as actress Jessica Brown-Findlay wanted to explore other acting avenues. She says was rarely recognized on the street as she appears quite differently in real life.

Jessica Brown-Findlay who plays Lady Sybil appears in the Winter's Tale in 2014, alongside Russell Crowe, Colin Farrell, Jennifer Connelly, and Will Smith.

Tom Branson (Allen Leech)

Tom is the former chauffeur who married Lady Sybil. Now a widower in the event of her death and the father of Lord and Lady Grantham's granddaughter, he lives in social limbo.

He becomes the manager of the Downton estate which assuages this problem somewhat but he still feels the awkwardness of being between floors even though the Grantham family have accepted him.

Like his character, Allen Leech is Irish. His parents wanted him to become an architect but stated they would support his decision to become an actor if he got a degree "just in case". He got a degree in Drama and Theater at Trinity College, Dublin.

He was overweight as a child and bullied at school. Acting helped him cope although he had no idea he could follow it as a profession until he was in his mid-teens.

He is a big fan of horseracing and as one of the show's heart-throbs, he admitted to once receiving half a bra from a fan!

Below Stairs

Charles Carson – Butler

Carson started working at Downton Abbey as a boy and has worked his way up to Butler, the most senior position within the house.

Carson takes his job very seriously and is strict about standards within the house.

He looks on Lady Mary as a surrogate daughter and is also close to Violet Crawley, both of whom long for a time gone by.

As a young man, Carson appeared on stage as part of a double act called "The Cheerful Charlies".

Along with other members of the household, Carson contracts the Spanish Flu, although he goes on to make a full recovery.

Fellowes based the character of Carson on retired butler Arthur Inch, who served as the principal advisor on the film "Gosford Park".

Jim Carter (Carson)

Jim has been an actor for over **30** years with a career spanning the stage, TV and the big screen.

He is married to the English actress, Imelda Staunton.

Jim says of acting, "I love that variety in my job. I could never be a butler in real life. Too much routine!"

Such is his commitment to acting, he has never earned a penny from doing anything else.

Jim has been a keen cyclist for over 55 years and regularly takes part in charity cycling events, including a 10 day cycle trip in Ghana in 2011.

Carter also has an Emmy nomination for Best Supporting Actor for his role in Downton Abbey.

Mrs. Hughes - Head Housekeeper

Elsie Hughes is the head housekeeper and in charge of all the female servants of the house.

Whilst she was working as head housemaid at the Abbey, she was courting a local farmer Joe Burns. She turned down his marriage proposal as she enjoyed her job and didn't want to leave. Years later, he returns to woo her again, but after dinner with him she decides she made the right decision and refuses a second proposal.

Mrs. Hughes is virtually the equal of Mr. Carson, and whilst she shares his sense of discipline in the running of the house, she is more flexible than him as times change around them.

At the end of the day you will often find Mrs. Hughes and Carson sharing confidences over a glass of sherry. As the only people downstairs of similar standing, it is not surprising that they share a certain allegiance to their work.

Although she is strict in her approach to running the household, Mrs. Hughes is kindhearted and cares about the staff beneath her. She often goes out of her way to help them out.

Phyllis Logan (Mrs. Hughes)

Executive producer Gareth Neame tells that they didn't offer the part of Mrs. Hughes to anyone else. "There is something about Phyllis' personality that lends itself to this character. She is the person you would go to in a crisis".

Jim Carter, says that she is 'the world's greatest hostess, always with a house full of guests'.

Phyllis is married to actor Kevin McNally who plays cantankerous Horace Bryant whose son, Major Bryant, gets housemaid Ethel pregnant.

Phyllis says she feels a real connection to the era of Downton Abbey due to the First World War. Her grandfather was killed just three days before the Armistice, when her father was only 17 months old. For Phyllis, the direct connection she holds with WWI still keeps the era firmly in her mind.

Phyllis thought Downton Abbey would have a modicum of success, but didn't think it would become the massive global hit that it has.

John Bates ("Mr. Bates") (Brendan Coyle)

John Bates is the valet to Robert Crawley. Due to an injury in the Boer war he walks with a limp and is treated poorly by most of the staff.

He is first married to Vera Bates, but doesn't love her, and in time he falls in love with Anna Smith (lady maid to Lady Mary) to whom he is happily married.

Brendan started his working life in his dad's butchers shop. It wasn't until after his father's death that he started to think about a change. He chose acting.

Julian Fellowes wrote the part of John Bates for Brendan. He says that he knew Brendan would have the capacity to portray Bates' bitter past without directly indicating it.

Brendan was recently in *Mojo* at the Harold Pinter Theatre in London's West End. It also starred Rupert Grint who played Ron Weasley in the Harry Potter films. Joanne Froggatt who plays his on-screen wife in Downton Abbey attended the opening night.

He is the great-nephew of England soccer great, Sir Matt Busby.

Anna Smith/Bates (Joanne Froggatt)

Anna is lady's maid to Lady Mary and holds one of the highest positions in the house. When Kemal Pamuk dies in Lady Mary's bed after a one night stand, it is Anna along with Lady Cora who move the body to avoid a scandal.

Anna thinks she has passed up the chance to marry and be happy, but she later falls in love and marries John Bates. Theirs is one of the most fondly considered relationships in the show.

Joanne has appeared on numerous British TV shows since starting her acting career. She appeared in soap opera *Coronation Street*, 1997-8. And one of her first performances was as a teenage prostitute on *The Bill*, a police soap opera.

Unlike many of the Downton Abbey cast, Joanne is originally from Yorkshire where the show is set.

She is particularly fond of her character Anna exclaiming, "She's just so lovely…..the kind of person I'd want as a friend".

Anna often appears tiny compared to her on-screen husband. She is 5'2". He is 6'2".

Thomas Barrow (Rob James-Collier)

Thomas is the scheming footman at Downton Abbey. He's a malicious gossip and loves to cause trouble.

He is the only gay character in the show. Although his sexuality is known to the servants, they keep quiet about it as it was an offence to be homosexual in England during the first half of the 20th century.

Thomas is played by Rob James-Collier. Prior to Downton Abbey, Rob also worked on long-running soap opera, Coronation Street. He has also worked as a catalog model.

He has two business degrees; one in business, the other in marketing.

Daisy Mason (Sophie McShera)

Daisy is the kitchen maid who has been brought on from a young girl who was so nervous she could hardly speak. She is now a young woman who works as second cook and has aspirations of her own.

In the second series she marries, rather reluctantly, former footman William who has been grievously injured in the war. On his death, she is befriended by his father who has no other children. Daisy forms part of a sweet subplot as she is mentored and guided by head cook, Mrs. Patmore and, more gently, by her father-in-law.

Sophie who plays the part of Daisy is also from Yorkshire. She will star in the Disney film *Cinderella* alongside Cate Blanchett and Helena Bonham Carter in 2015.

Historical events depicted in Downton Abbey

The Sinking of the Titanic

The first series opens with the news that the heir to the Crawley Estate has been lost aboard the Titanic. The year is 1912 and the seemingly unsinkable ship was on its maiden voyage to New York.

The Titanic struck the iceberg at 11.40pm on the evening of 14ᵗʰ April 1912. Less than 3 hours later, at 2.20am, she broke apart and sank beneath the waves with a loss of around 1,500 lives.

Much has always been made of the lack of lifeboats aboard the Titanic. There were too few to cope with a disaster on the scale of that which befell it that night. However, many lifeboats were launched barely half-full, as staff were unsure of the capacity of each lifeboat.

Third class passengers were largely left to fend for themselves. Many were trapped below stairs and the loss of lives was felt largest amongst this group.

The Titanic sank to a depth of 12,600 feet and remains there to this day.

On the night the ship sank, there were a total of 6 iceberg warnings. The ship continued at full steam despite this, its Captain anxious to arrive on its maiden voyage ahead of time.

World War I

World War I broke out on the 28ᵗʰ July 1914 and lasted until Armistice Day on the 11ᵗʰ November 1918.

Before World War II, it was known simply as "The Great War" or the "World War". After World War II broke out, it became known as World War I. In America, it is often referred to as the European War.

65 million men from over 30 countries fought in WWI. Of those 65 million, nearly 10 million lost their lives.

The phrase 'dogfights' originated from WWI. This was when a pilot had to turn off his airplane engine when turning quickly in the air to avoid stalling. When the engines were turned back on, they sounded like dogs barking.

Thousands of soldiers were left disabled and disfigured by their injuries. Reconstructive surgery helped some, but many simply had to wear masks.

Lady Almina, the Countess of Carnarvon, lived at Highclere Castle during the turn of the century and through World War I, and like Lady Cora, she allowed her house to be turned into a hospital for wounded soldiers, running it at her own expense.

WWI is numbered as the sixth deadliest war in world history.

Conclusion

Period dramas never seem to lose their fascination and Downton Abbey is no exception.

Now in its fourth series, its number of fans continue to grow.

Its popularity is hard to pinpoint, but perhaps it lies in the simpler way of life that existed at the turn of the 20th century.

It was a tough way of life for those born without privilege and destined for jobs in service, although it was equally tough for women born into a family that has to do its utmost to stay on the right side of the social tracks.

Married young into partnerships that were often nothing more than deals to keep titles and money in the family, these young women would have to put aside any thoughts of pursuing their own dreams.

Whatever its popularity, it is a world away from the modern society that we now live in. Perhaps this is where its true appeal lies, that it provides us with a form of escapism from our own lives. Back to a time where everyone knew their role and place in life.

Who knows its charm, we only know it works.

Don't Forget to Claim Your Free Gift!

As a "thank you" for purchasing this book I want to give you a gift. It is 100% absolutely free.

Please go to http://fandomkindlebooks.com/downton-abbey-bonus/ to discover more fascinating facts about Downton Abbey and the smash hit BBC TV series.

Other Books from Green Hills Press

Available on Kindle and in paperback on Amazon:

Books in the Paleo Kitchen and Health Series

*Paleo Bacon Cookbook: Lose Weight * Get Healthy * Eat Bacon*

Paleo Cravings: Your Favorite Comfort Foods Made Paleo

Paleo Easter Cookbook: Fast and Easy Recipes for Busy Moms

Paleo Party Food Cookbook: Make Your Friends Love You With Delicious & Healthy Party Food!

Paleo Pizza Cookbook: Lose Weight and Get Healthy by Eating the Food You Love

Paleo Valentine's Day Cookbook: Quick, Easy Recipes That Will Melt Your Lover's Heart

Simple Easy Paleo: Fast Fabulous Paleo Recipes with 5 Ingredients or Less

Coconut Health Made Simple: Coconut Oil Cures & Health Hacks to Lose Weight, Lower Cholesterol, Improve Your Memory, Hair, & Skin

Break Free From Emotional Eating: Stop Overeating and Start Losing Weight

Don't delay! Check them out today!

6554111R00024

Printed in Germany
by Amazon Distribution
GmbH, Leipzig